English Phonics Resource Guide

Pam Schiller

A Division of The McGraw-Hill Companies

Columbus, Ohio

www.sra4kids.com

SRA/McGraw-Hill

A Division of The **McGraw-Hill** *Companies*

Send all inquiries to:
SRA/McGraw-Hill
8787 Orion Place
Columbus, OH 43240-4027

Printed in the United States of America.

ISBN 0-07-572273-9

1 2 3 4 5 6 7 8 9 VIC 07 06 05 04 03 02

Table of Contents

Introduction

Philosophy

One of the goals of early-childhood education is to help children develop their ability to communicate. At the pre-kindergarten level, this effort focuses on the development of oral language skills and an awareness of the relationship between oral and written language. Children must develop an appreciation for language before they focus on the specific skills required for reading.

Reading requires the use of many processes, including word configuration, context clue identification, sight word recognition, language pattern understanding, and phonetic analysis. Phonics is one of several tools used in reading. Most educators now recognize that some children need more direct instruction in phonics and that all children need phonics experience in meaningful contexts that occur naturally in daily routines and lessons.

Support from Brain Research

From emerging neuroscience research we have learned that the first few years of life lay the foundation for reading skills in later years. Between the fourth and eighth months of life, a child's brain will develop what is called a native language map. A neuron will be assigned to every sound in the native language. Argue as we may about when phonics should be introduced, it is clear from the research that infants are already ahead of us.

This is why talking and reading to infants is so crucial. The more verbal language a child is exposed to in his or her early years, the greater his or her ability to discriminate among sounds and the broader his or her vocabulary. Both skills are predictors of reading success.

There is no absolute timetable for learning how to read. Normal ranges can vary by as much as three years. Several experts recommend that providing rich experiences for brain development and allowing the children to formulate their own schedules is still the best practice.

A Developmental Perspective

To understand how language and reading develop, it is helpful to take a look at how children develop. It takes most infants two years to master the skills that lead to speaking. These two years are marked by tremendous physical and mental growth. An infant's sense of hearing matures around the fifth month. Neural connections for the sounds in an infant's native language are assigned between the fourth and eighth months of life. Between the ages of two and six, a child's wiring for vision matures, small-muscle coordination is achieved, and critical thinking skills emerge. The child becomes capable of longer periods of attention and is rapidly developing a more sophisticated vocabulary.

Before a child can learn to read, the oral, visual, and auditory groundwork must be in place—a number of maturational and experiential benchmarks have to be achieved. He or she must become familiar with language in general. An environment rich in language of all types provides modeling for the development of speech. These early years are filled with achievements and experiences that provide the foundation for the child's future development. The child's early experiences include numerous language-building events: being spoken to, being read to, listening to adult speech, modeling the production of sounds, and being rewarded with many celebrations of approximations of speech, such as cooing and babbling, along the way. During this time, the more the child is spoken to and read to and the greater his or her exposure to oral language is, the more prepared he or she is to take the next step toward reading.

During this time, children need multiple and repetitive opportunities to play with language (e.g., rhyming, singing, looking for patterns) before they begin the more formal process of mastering the mechanics of reading (i.e. matching sounds with symbols). Language is a relatively new toy that needs plenty of play and exploration. They need opportunities to talk and opportunities for writing attempts. As they are taking these steps toward literacy, they need positive reinforcement; they need to celebrate their milestones and accomplishments.

Basic Principles of Emergent Literacy

Emergent literacy is a term used to describe the beginnings of oral and written language proficiency. According to research, the basic principles of emergent literacy include the following:

1. It is a social process. It occurs in the context of children's interactions with other children and adults.
2. Literacy begins at birth. From an infant's first observations of human behavior and his or her resulting imitations of adult sounds and social cues, literacy is developing.
3. All aspects of literacy—listening, speaking, reading, writing and thinking—develop interdependently.
4. Literacy develops along a continuum similar to intellectual and physical growth. Children will develop literacy at their own pace. Slow progress often indicates that internalization is occurring.

Realistic Expectations

Each child is unique. Children are all individuals based on their genetic make-up and their environmental influences. However, there are some general expectations for specific age-related accomplishments that have emerged from years of research, observation, and study.

Below is a list of age-related accomplishments published in *Preventing Reading Difficulties in Young Children* (Catherine E. Snow, M. Susan Burns, and Peg Griffin, *eds.*; National Academy Press, 1998). Bear in mind that the timing of these accomplishments is contingent on maturational and experiential differences among children.

Three- to Four-Year-Old Accomplishments

- Knows that alphabet letters are a special category of visual graphics that can be individually named.
- Recognizes print in the local environment.
- Understands that different text forms are used for different functions of print (e.g., a list for groceries is different than the list on a menu).
- Pays attention to separable and repeating sound in language (e.g., in Peter, Peter, Pumpkin Eater: Peter Eater).
- Uses new vocabulary and grammatical constructions in own speech.
- Understands and follows oral directions.
- Is sensitive to some sequences of events in stories.
- Shows an interest in books and reading.
- While listening to a story, connects information and events to real-life experiences.
- Questions and comments demonstrate some comprehension of a story's literal meaning.
- Displays reading and writing attempts and calls attention to self: "Look at my story."
- Identifies about 10 alphabet letters, especially those from own name.
- Writes (scribbles) message as part of playful activity.
- Attempts to attend to the beginning or rhyming sound in salient words.

Using the English Phonics Resource Guide

This book is filled with songs, stories, finger plays, and rhymes that encourage children to enjoy the sounds of language. As children become accustomed to the rhythm and patterns of language, they will develop the auditory skills to prepare them for more formal reading instruction. Allowing time and opportunities for this maturation experience will help ensure that children develop a disposition (desire) to read. Disposition is as important as a skill because, no matter how well children may be able to read, they will not read if they do not have the motivation to read.

To learn how to read successfully, children must first have the overall picture of what reading is about. They will need to understand that written words have meaning and words can be represented by printed symbols (letters). They must have the desire to tackle the challenge of distinguishing sounds and recognizing the discrete differences in letter shapes. This book offers activities and suggestions to help children develop both the big picture and the skills they will need to read.

Phonics Activities

This section contains name stories, songs, poems, finger plays, tongue twisters, and small-group activities that you can use to introduce various sound-symbol relationships.

Word Lists

Word Lists, which include Dolch words, suggest simple, familiar words that are useful when introducing basic phonics concepts. For example, *cat, cave,* and *cow*, words that begin with the letter **C,** follow the consonant-vowel-consonant-vowel pattern, and are picturable.

Using the Resource Guide

The guide includes activities that will build a wide range of oral language and phonics skills. A suggested sequence of activities is listed below.

1. Choose a letter of the alphabet.
2. Read the corresponding name story.

3. At this point, you might decide that you want to use a Small-Group Activity. These activities and experiences may be more beneficial to the children if they are used for a few consecutive days and then repeated in a week or two.
4. You can use a tongue twister to reinforce the sound-symbol relationship.
5. This is another good time to use a Small-Group Activity.
6. Introduce the consonant-vowel-consonant pattern when the children are ready.

Phonics Activities

Amy—Name Story

Amy's birthday is in August. She likes animals, especially apes and antelopes. Amy's favorite foods are apples and almonds. Anita is Amy's best friend. They think it's fun to run in the backyard waving their arms around. One day, Amy would like to be an accountant like her father Adam.

I'm a Little Acorn Brown — Song

I'm a little acorn brown,
Lying on the cold, cold ground.
Everyone walks over me,
That is why I'm cracked you see.
I'm a nut. *(clap, clap)*
In a rut. *(clap, clap)*
I'm a nut. *(clap, clap)*
In a rut. *(clap, clap)*

April Fool! — Poem

Little bears have three feet,
Little birds have four.
Little cats have two feet
And boys and girls have more.

Do you believe my story?
Do you think it's wrong?
I tell it only once a year,
When April comes along!

April — Finger Play

Two little clouds one April day
(Hold both hands in fists.)

Went sailing across the sky.
(Move fist from left to right.)

They went so fast that they bumped their heads
(Bump fists together.)

And both began to cry.
(Point to eyes.)

The big round sun came out and said,
(Make circle with arms.)

"Oh, never mind, my dears,

I'll send all my sunbeams down
(Wiggle fingers downward like rain.)

To dry your fallen tears."

Tongue Twister

Angry apes ate. *(Say three times quickly.)*

Small-Group Activities

Ace Concentration

Remove the aces from two decks of cards. Lay the aces facedown and invite the children to play.

Acorns

Have the children count acorns into numbered tubs. If real acorns aren't available, draw some for the children to count.

Aiming

Challenge the children to stand several feet away from a service bell and try to ring it using a beanbag you have provided.

April Showers

Ask the children to draw pictures of April Showers using drawing paper and white crayons. Encourage the children to make raindrops on the paper then go over them with blue watercolors.

Aviators

Have children role-play being aviators using props you have provided.

Ben—Name Story

Ben was born in Cambodia. He has lots of building blocks and likes to build bridges. Barney is his pet hamster. Barney lives in a big blue cage in Ben's room. Before school, Ben fills Barney's bowl with fresh water. After school, Ben takes Barney to the backyard so he can bask in the sun and browse on the dandelions.

Baby Bumblebee — Song

I caught myself a baby bumblebee.
Won't my mommy be so proud of me.
I caught myself a baby bumblebee.
Ouch! It stung me.
I'm talking to my baby bumblebee.
Won't my mommy be so proud of me.
I'm talking to my baby bumblebee.
"Oh," he said, "I'm sorry."
I'm letting go my baby bumblebee.
Won't my mommy be so proud of me.
I'm letting go my baby bumblebee.
Look he's happy to be free!

Little Boy Blue — Poem

Little Boy Blue, come blow your horn,
The sheep are in the meadow, the cow's in the corn.
But where is the boy who looks after the sheep?
He's under a haystack, fast asleep.

Five Little Bells — Finger Play

Five little bells hanging in a row
(Hold up five fingers.)

The first bell said, "Ring me slow."
(Wiggle thumb.)

The second bell said, "Ring me fast."
(Wiggle index finger.)

The third bell said, "Ring me last."
(Wiggle middle finger.)

The fourth bell said, "I won't ring."
(Wiggle ring finger.)

The fifth bell said, "I'd rather sing."
(Wiggle little finger.)

Tongue Twister

A big, blind, black bear (*Say three times quickly.*)

Small-Group Activities

Baby Bumblebee

Cut a yellow egg carton into six sections of two humps. Use a black marker to draw stripes. Glue on paper or roll-eyes. Use yellow chenille wires for side wings. Use black chenille wires for antennae and stingers. Sing the song "Baby Bumblebee."

Balance a Beanbag Backwards

Practice walking a straight line while balancing a beanbag on your head. Then try it walking backwards.

Blow Bubbles

Put a small amount of water and liquid detergent into a margarine tub or wash tub. Add a few drops of glycerin to make the bubbles stronger and/or food coloring for variety. Provide plastic straws for blowing.

Build the Biggest Building

Give each of two groups of children the same number of blocks. Have them work together to see which group can build the biggest building.

Burst a Balloon

Hold a balloon relay. In turn, each child runs to a balloon and sits on it to burst it.

C

Can—Name Story

Can comes from Thailand. She looks for caterpillars in the cornstalks on her family's farm in California. She can count to 100. Can's family likes to go camping and catch fish. Can thinks she could be the captain of a ship when she grows up, or maybe a chef. Her pet is a yellow canary called Candy.

Clap Your Hands — Song

(Suit movements to words.)

Clap your hands 1-2-3.
Clap your hands just like me.
Wiggle your hands 1-2-3.
Wiggle your hands just like me.

Clickety, Clickety, Clack — Poem

Clickety, clickety, clack.
Clickety, clickety, clack.
Clickety, clickety, clickety, clickety,
Clickety, clickety, clack.

(Make a train. Add more children at the end of each verse.)

Caterpillar — Finger Play

"Who's that tickling my back?" asked the wall. *(Crawl fingers up arm.)*

"Me," said a small caterpillar, "I'm learning to crawl."

Tongue Twister

Crisp crusts (*Say three times quickly.*)

Small-Group Activities

Cars on a Curve

On a large sheet of butcher paper, draw a road with curves. Provide small cars and trucks so the children can practice guiding their cars around the curves.

Collage Creation

Provide small paper shapes in various colors for the children to use to create a collage.

Cookie Cutters and Clay

Roll out clay and create with cookie cutters!

Come to the Clinic

Set up a Center area as a clinic or doctor's office. Supply first-aid materials such as tape, bandages, and cotton balls so the children can pretend to visit a clinic.

Cut from a Catalog

Collect old catalogs. Have the children cut out pictures and sort them into categories, for example, clothes, toys, jewelry, furniture.

Dario—Name Story

Dario's birthday is in December, and he desperately wants a dog. If he had a dog, they would do everything together. His best friend David has a dog named Daisy. She doesn't bark or jump, but she does drool. Dario wants a dog just like Daisy, who likes to go on drives and doesn't chew on his drawings.

Down by the Station

Song

Down by the station
Early in the morning,
See the little puffer-bellies
All in a row.
See the engine driver
Pull the little throttle.
Puff, puff! Toot, toot!
Off we go.

Downy Duck

Poem

One day I saw a downy duck
With feathers on his back;
I said, "Good morning, downy duck."
And he said, "Quack, quack, quack."

My Doll

Finger Play

This is how my doll walks,
(Walk around with stiff arms and legs.)

This is how it walks, you see?
This is how my doll talks, *(Bend at waist.)*
This is how it talks, you see?

Tongue Twister

Dizzy dancing Dan (*Say three times quickly.*)

Small-Group Activities

Daily Diary

Make a class chart of each day's events. At the end of each month, compile the pages and bind into a book. Place the Daily Diary of the month in the Library Center for all of the children to enjoy.

Delicious Dessert Day

Discuss and list the children's favorite desserts. Then have the children draw their favorite desserts and dictate recipes.

Do a Donut Dance

Divide the class into two groups and form two circles, one inside the other. The children can dance or skip around in the circles to music.

Doodle Design

Draw large doodles and have children use crayons or markers to fill in each space with a different color or design.

Duck and Dodge

Build an obstacle course outdoors using such things as cones, hula hoops, and chairs. The children will duck and dodge as they go around, under, over, and through.

Enola—Name Story

Enola thinks the best pet would be an elephant. If she had one, she'd name it Edward and take him everywhere she went. Even if she was eating, Edward would be with her, eating too. Every day she asks for an elephant, but either her mother or father says no. Enola is beginning to wonder if she's ever going to get an elephant.

Eensy Weensy Spider — Song

The eensy weensy spider went up the waterspout.
(Crawl fingers up arm.)
Down came the rain and washed the spider out.
(Move hands across front of body.)
Out came the sun and dried up all the rain.
(Hold hands spread above head.)
The eensy weensy spider went up the spout again.
(Crawl fingers up arm.)

Where Do You Wear Your Ears? — Poem

Where do you wear your ears?
Underneath your hat?
Where do you wear your ears?
Yes, ma'am, just like that.
Where do you wear your ears?
Say where, you sweet, sweet child.
Where do you wear your ears?
On both ends of my smile!

Little Easter Rabbit — Finger Play

Little Easter Rabbit goes hip, hop, hip,
(Hop hand.)
See how his ears go flip, flop, flip.
(Hold hands by ears and flop them.)
See how his eyes go blink, blink, blink.
(Blink eyes.)
See how his nose goes twink, twink, twink.
(Wiggle nose.)
Pet his white coat, so soft and furry,
(Stroke arm.)
Hip, hop, hip—he's off in a hurry.
(Hop hand away.)

Tongue Twister

Edith eats eggs. (*Say three times quickly.*)

Small-Group Activities

Each Is Equal

Assign helpers to give equal servings of juice and cookies to everyone.

Easel Event

Make an event of trying some new metallic or fluorescent colors at the easel today.

Easter Bonnets

Make and decorate paper plate hats.

Easy Eats

Provide finger foods for lunch or a snack.

Emergency

Teach the children to dial 911 in an emergency. Discuss what an emergency involves.

Frank—Name Story

Frank lives in Florida. Fall is his favorite time of year. He likes to fish, fly toy airplanes, and play fetch with his dog Fido. Frank's father flies real planes for a living. His mother Flora sells flowers, frames, and faucets at the family store. Frank would like to own his own farm when he grows up.

Five Little Speckled Frogs

Song

(Five children sit in a row, and the other children sit in a circle around them. All children act out the words to the song.)

Five Little Speckled Frogs
(Hold up five fingers.)
Sitting on a speckled log
Eating some most delicious bugs.
(Pretend to eat bugs.)
Yum! Yum!
One jumped into the pool,
(One child from center jumps back into the circle.)
Where it was nice and cool.
(*Cross arms over chest and shiver.*)
Now there are four little speckled frogs.
Burr-ump!

(Repeat, counting down, until there are no little speckled frogs.)

Floppy Rag Doll

Poem

(Suit actions to words.)

Flop your arms, flop your feet,
Let your hand go free.
You're the floppiest rag doll
I am ever going to see.

Ten Little Fingers

Finger Play

I have ten little fingers
(Hold up ten fingers.)
And they all belong to me.
(Point to self.)
I can make them do things
(Wiggle fingers.)
Do you want to see?
(Tilt head.)
I can make them point
(Point.)
I can make them hold.
(Hold fingertips together.)
I can make them dance
(Dance fingers on arm.)
And then make them fold.
(Fold hands in lap.)

Tongue Twister

Fresh fish (*Say three times quickly.*)

Small-Group Activities

Fast Feet

Plan outdoor races using locomotor skills. Practice walking, running, hopping, or jumping.

Field Trip to a Fire Station

Take a field trip to the local fire station. Afterwards write a thank-you letter.

Flying Disk Fun

Play with a flying disk in a school field.

Fun on the Farm

Build a farm from blocks and plastic farm animals.

Fun with My Friend

Have the children draw a picture of a favorite thing to do with a friend.

Guadalupe—Name Story

Guadalupe goes to school in Galveston. She gets good grades, even though she giggles a lot. Her brother Gaspar loves to eat grapes while his pet goat grazes on grass. Guadalupe wants to be a gardener because they get to work with their hands and wear gloves. Gaspar wants to own a grocery so he'll always have grapes.

Goodnight

Song

Goodnight ladies, good night gentlemen,
Goodnight everyone,
It's time to say good-bye.

Goldilocks, Goldilocks

Poem

Goldilocks, Goldilocks, turn around.
(Turn around.)
Goldilocks, Goldilocks, touch the ground.
(Touch the ground.)
Goldilocks, Goldilocks, knock on the door.
(Knock with hand.)
Goldilocks, Goldilocks, eat some porridge.
(Pretend to eat porridge.)
Goldilocks, Goldilocks, have a seat.
(Squat.)
Goldilocks, Goldilocks, go to sleep.
(Put head on folded hands.)
Goldilocks, Goldilocks, run, run, run.
(Run off paper and back to beginning.)

Making a Garden

Finger Play

(Suit actions to words.)

Dig, dig, dig,
Rake just so.
Plant the seeds,
Watch them grow.

Chop, chop, chop,
Pull up the weeds.
Sun and rain
My garden needs.

Up, up, up,
Green stems climb.
Open wide,
It's blossom time!

Tongue Twister

Gray geese (*Say three times quickly.*)

Small-Group Activities

Galloping in the Green Grass

Practice galloping outside in the grass. Discuss how horses graze in the grass.

Get a Goal!

Let the children dribble a soccer ball with their feet and kick it to make a goal.

Go to the Garage

Talk about parking garages—single garages and multilevel garages. Let the children use blocks and ramps to build a garage.

Grandparents Are Great!

Discuss how special grandparents are, and encourage the children to share special memories and/or feelings about their grandparents.

Growing Grass

Put a small sponge in a flat tray of water and sprinkle grass seeds on the sponge. Keep the sponge moist. In a few days the seeds will sprout.

Hasani—Name Story

Hasani is from Africa. Now he lives in Houston. He has one brother and two sisters. His father helps build houses. Hasani likes hamburgers and hot dogs, but not ham. His hair hangs in his eyes, making him shake his head. However, he won't let his mother cut it for him. "How silly, Hasani!" his mother says.

If You're Happy and You Know It — Song

If you're happy and you know it, clap your hands
If you're happy and you know it, clap your hands
If you're happy and you know, then your face
will surely show it
If you're happy and you know it, clap your hands.

(Continue with stomp your feet, shout hooray, *and any other actions you desire.)*

Hot-Cross Buns! — Poem

Hot-cross buns!
Hot-cross buns!
One a penny, two a penny,
Hot-cross buns!

Hot-cross buns!
Hot-cross buns!
If ye have no daughters,
Give them to your sons.

My Head — Finger Play

(Suit actions to words.)

This is the circle that is my head.
This is my mouth with which words are said.
These are my eyes with which I see.
This is my nose that is part of me.
This is the hair that grows on my head,
And this is my hat I wear on my head.

Tongue Twister

A huge hush (*Say three times quickly.*)

Small-Group Activities

Habits and Habitats

Display several books and pictures about animals. Discuss the environment in which the animals live and any unusual characteristics. Then create a comparison chart or word web with the children.

Heart Hopscotch

With sidewalk chalk, draw a hopscotch with heart shapes. The children can toss a heart-shaped piece of wood instead of a stone.

Helping at Home

Brainstorm jobs and chores that must be done at home to keep a house clean, safe, and healthy. Provide props used for these jobs, and let the children role-play household jobs such as dusting, sweeping, and washing.

Hit the Hole

Suspend a large hoop from the ceiling and let the children toss sponge balls through the hole.

Hooray for Hobbies

Discuss hobbies and make a list of hobbies the children have or would like to have.

I

Ima—Name Story

Ima moved to Idaho from Japan. When she has an important idea, she tells it to her identical twin Imaki. Ima and Imaki like to investigate things. They like to imagine they are searching for hidden or buried treasure. It is important to be patient when looking for clues. Maybe they will be private investigators.

I Have Something in My Pocket

Song

I have something in my pocket
It belongs across my face
I keep it very close at hand
In a most convenient place.
I bet you could guess it
If you guessed a long long while
So I'll take it out and put it on
It's a great big happy SMILE!

Ice Cream

Poem

I scream.
You scream.
We all scream for ice cream.

Five Ice-Cream Cones

Finger Play

Pam Schiller

(Suit actions to words.)

Five ice-cream cones from the ice-cream store,
Mommy takes strawberry now there are four,
Daddy takes chocolate which leaves only three
Will there be any ice cream for me?
Sam says he'll have chocolate like Dad
Now there are only two cones to be had.
I have an idea I'm not sure they'll agree
I think I'll take both cones just for me.

Tongue Twister

Izzy is itchy. (*Say three times quickly.*)

Small-Group Activities

I Am the Greatest

Encourage the children to tell what they think they do best. If a child is shy, let the other children suggest something wonderful about the child.

Ice Painting

Fill an ice tray with water and place a stick in each crate. After the ice freezes, give one to each child to use as a brush. Provide saltshakers filled with dry tempera paint. Show the children how to sprinkle it on their papers and then use their ice paintbrush to draw a picture or design.

I.D. Card

Give each child a photocopy of their photo and an index card. Have them glue the photo onto the card and make a fingerprint on the card. Next, ask them to write their names on the card. Finally, have them dictate a sentence about themselves and write it on the card.

Itsy Bitsy Spider

Encourage the children to think of things they have to practice doing. Help them make an Itsy Bitsy Spider out of chenille wires and keep it nearby to serve as a reminder to keep on trying.

Islands

Ask the children to construct islands of clay in the water play table.

Jacy—Name Story

Jacy is a Native American whose name means *Moon*. He likes to jump and jiggle. Jacy likes just jelly on his toast. Juice is his favorite drink. He keeps all of his money in a jar so he can buy his sister a jump rope and some jacks for her birthday in January. His favorite thing at school is the jungle gym.

Johnny Works with One Hammer Song

Johnny works with one hammer,
One hammer, one hammer.
(Make hammering motion with right hand.)
Johnny works with one hammer,
Then he works with two.

(Additional verses:)
Johnny works with two hammers, . . .
(Motion with left and right hands.)
Johnny works with three hammers, . . .
(Motion with both hands and right foot.)
Johnny works with four hammers, . . .
(Motion with both hands and both feet.)
Johnny works with five hammers, . . .
(Motion with both hands and feet and with head.)
Then he goes to bed.

Jack and Jill Poem

Jack and Jill went up the hill
To fetch a pail of water.
Jack fell down
And broke his crown
And Jill came tumbling after.

Jack, Jack Finger Play

Jack, Jack, down you go,
(Crouch down low.)
Down in your box, down so low.
Jack, Jack, there goes the top.
(Pop up.)
Quickly now, up you pop.

Tongue Twister

Just jump, John! (*Say three times quickly.*)

Small-Group Activities

Jack and Jill

Say the nursery rhyme "Jack and Jill." Have children role-play the parts. Provide a pail for a prop.

Join the Joints

Provide paper and elongated oval patterns for arms and legs. Have the children trace and cut ovals. Then have them connect arms and legs with brads. Discuss how our bodies bend and move at the joints—shoulder, elbow, wrist, hip, knee, and ankle. Let the children move their own joints and the ones they made.

Join Us for Juice and Jelly

Serve snacks of juice and jelly on soda crackers or graham crackers.

Jump for Joy!

Have the children form a circle and squat. Say words very slowly. The children will "jump for joy" when they hear a word that begins with the letter **J**.

Just Junk

Provide a variety of junk items such as buttons, straws, wood, and cardboard. Have the children glue junk together to create "just junk."

Katie—Name Story

Katie was born in Kansas. If she could have anything in the world, it would be a kangaroo. She likes the way they kick. Katie learned in school that a baby goat is a kid. She is looking forward to starting kindergarten. Katie loves peas, but she doesn't like kidney beans. She puts ketchup on everything.

Kookaburra

Song

Kookaburra sits in the old gum tree-ee
Merry, merry king of the bush is hee-ee.
Laugh, Kookaburra. Laugh, Kookaburra,
How fun your life must be!

Kookaburra sits in the old gum tree-ee
Kissing all the monkeys he can see-ee.
Stop, Kookaburra! Stop, Kookaburra!
That's no monkey, that's me!

Kookaburra sits in the old gum tree-ee.
Eating all the gumdrops he can see-ee.
Stop, Kookaburra! Stop, Kookaburra!
Leave a few for me!

Hickory, Dickory Dock

Poem

Hickory, dickory dock.
The mouse ran up the clock.
The clock struck one,
The mouse ran down.
Hickory dickory dock.

Kangaroo

Finger Play

Jump, jump, jump,
(Move right fist up and down.)
Goes the kangaroo.
I thought there was one,
(Hold up one, then two fingers.)
But I see there are two.
The mother takes her baby
(Place thumb inside palm of opposite hand.)
Along in a pouch,
Where he can nap
Like a baby on a couch.
(Rest head on hands.)

Tongue Twister

Karate kicking (*Say three times quickly.*)

Small-Group Activities

Keep the Keys

Provide a variety of keys and locks that fit. Have the children experiment with keys to find the locks that match.

Put the Kettle On

Bring a tea kettle to show children what a kettle is. Read the nursery rhyme "Polly, Put the Kettle On." Demonstrate what a kettle does when water boils.

Kids in the Kitchen

Set up a kitchen area for dramatic play with a stove, refrigerator, sink, and dishes. Encourage the children to role-play jobs in the kitchen at home or at a restaurant. Let children prepare a simple snack in their kitchen.

Kit for Kids

Let the children organize tools and accessories in a toolbox. Then let them safely use the tools to build something.

Kazoos of All Kinds

Provide inexpensive plastic kazoos for the children to play. You can make one by putting waxed paper over one end of an empty toilet-tissue roll with a rubber band.

Lu—Name Story

Lu is from Vietnam. His family moved to Lubbock when he was little. His favorite animal at the zoo is the llama. He likes to listen to music and swim in the lake. When Lu's feeling lazy, he lies on the sofa and loafs around the living room. He owns a pet lizard named Lucky.

Little Rabbit

Song

In a cabin in the woods,
Little man by his window stood.
Saw a rabbit hopping by
Knocking at his door.
"Help me! Help me! Help me!" he cried.
"I'm so tired—can I come inside?"
Little Rabbit come inside
Safely to abide.

I Love You Little

Poem

I love you little,
I love you lots,
My love for you would fill ten pots,
Fifteen buckets,
Sixteen cans,
Three teacups,
And four dishpans.

I Look in the Mirror

Finger Play

I look in the mirror
(Hold hand up like a mirror.)
And what do I see?
I see a laughing face
(Make a laughing face.)
Happy as can be.

I look in the mirror
(Hold hand up like a mirror.)
And what do I see?
I see a laughing face
(Laugh and point to self.)
Laughing at me.

Tongue Twister

Lumpy, little lemons (*Say three times quickly.*)

Small-Group Activities

Lace Is Lovely

Provide a variety of lace scraps so the children can create a picture or special card for a special person.

Leader or Last in Line

Assign special duties to the children who are the leader and the last in line. This makes both places special and also brings continuity to your class line.

Learn a Lullaby

Provide lullaby music for the children to listen to. Discuss what a lullaby is and when you might hear or sing one. Have the children learn a lullaby together.

Long Leaps

Put masking tape strips on the floor. Have the children stand at the end of the tape and safely leap as far as they can.

Lots of Links

Provide paper strips, about 6" long, in a variety of colors. The children can make loops and interlock them to make a long chain.

Manuela—Name Story

Manuela is from Mexico. She lives in Minneapolis with her family. Manuela thinks the monkeys at the zoo are funny. Her birthday is in May, and she wants a music box and some money for her piggy bank. She wanted a monkey, but her mother said no. Maybe she'll get enough money to buy her own monkey.

Mister Moon

Song

O Mister Moon, Moon,
Bright and shiny Moon,
Won't you please
Shine down on me?

O Mister Moon, Moon,
Bright and shiny Moon,
Won't you please
Set me fancy free?
I'd like to linger
But I've got to run,
Mama's callin',
"Baby, get your homework done!"

O Mister Moon, Moon,
Bright and shiny Moon,
Won't you please
Shine down on me?
Talk about your shine on,
Please shine down on me.

I Measure Myself

Finger Play

(Suit actions to words.)

I measure myself from my head to my toes.
I measure my arms, starting right by my nose.
I measure my legs and I measure me all.
I measure to see if I'm growing tall.

Early Morning

Poem

The moon on the one hand,
the dawn on the other;
The moon is my sister,
the dawn is my brother.
The moon on my left hand,
the dawn on my right:
My brother, good morning:
my sister, good night.

Tongue Twister

Monkey money (*Say three times quickly.*)

Small-Group Activities

Markers Are Marvelous!

Tape two different colored markers together. Make up several different pairs. Let the children draw on a large white sheet with the markers. They'll think it's marvelous.

Meet Me at the Market

Discuss what a market is and that many are outdoors. Let each child draw what he or she would buy at the market and make a class book.

Make It with Magazines

Provide a variety of magazines so the children can cut out pictures to create their own collages.

Marching to Music

Play marching music and march to the beat. Children could play instruments as they march and pretend to be in a parade.

Man in the Moon

Read about and discuss why it looks like there is a face on the moon. Let the children paint a large moon shape and add the features of a face.

Nicole—Name Story

Nicole's birthday is in November. She asked for a pet newt. Nicole had even picked out names for a newt, Nina if it's a girl newt or Nate if it's a boy newt. Nicole had been saving her nickels, but she realized that wasn't nearly enough for a newt. At her ninth birthday party, Nicole noticed a navy box. She lifted the lid and, without a noise, out climbed her new newt!

I'm a Nut

Song

I'm a little acorn, small and round
Lying on the cold, cold ground.
Everyone walks over me,
That is why I'm cracked you see.
I'm a nut! (*click, click*)
I'm a nut! (*click, click*)
I'm a nut! (*click, click*)

Birdie, Birdie, Where Is Your Nest?

Poem

Birdie, birdie, where is your nest?
Birdie, birdie, where is your nest?
Birdie, birdie, where is your nest?
In the tree that I love best.

Cozy Little Nest

Finger Play

If I were a bird
(Hook thumbs together and fly hands around.)
I'd sing a song
And fly around
The whole day long.
And when it was dark
I'd go to rest
Up in my cozy
(Cup hands to form a nest.)
Little nest.

Tongue Twister

Not now, Nana (*Say three times quickly.*)

Small-Group Activities

Nibble on Nectarines

Provide nectarines and peaches for the children to sample. Compare the taste of a nectarine with that of a peach. Make a graph of preferences.

It's Neat to Be Nice

Discuss the positives of being kind or nice to others. Have each child draw a picture and dictate a sentence describing opportunities to show kindness.

Nifty Needlework

Trace simple designs on 8" squares of burlap. Let the children stitch around the designs with large, blunt needles and yarn.

N for a Nose

Draw a capital letter **N** in the center of 9" x 12" sheets of construction paper. Have children draw faces around the letter, adding a mouth, eyes, and hair.

Name the Noises

Make a tape of everyday household noises. Provide a picture to go with each one. Have the children match the picture to the noise they hear.

O

Olaf—Name Story

Olaf was born in Norway. When Olaf was one, his family moved to Ohio. They live on a farm where they have ostriches and oxen. Olaf often helps with the oats and onions they grow. Olaf wishes that they could grow olives. At night, Olaf listens for the owl that lives in their old oak tree that he calls Oscar.

Old MacDonald Had a Farm

Song

Old MacDonald had a farm,
E-I-E-I-O.
And on this farm she had a cow,
E-I-E-I-O.
With a moo, moo here,
And a moo, moo there,
Here a moo, there a moo,
Everywhere a moo, moo.
Old MacDonald had a farm,
E-I-E-I-O!

(Additional verses:)
Pig – oink, oink
Cat – meow, meow
Dog – bow-wow
Horse – neigh, neigh

The Sun Overhead

Poem

Over there the sun gets up
And marches all the day.
At noon it stands just overhead,
And at night it goes away.

Ocean Shell

Finger Play

I found a great big shell one day, upon the ocean floor.
(Cup hands as if holding a shell.)
I held it close up to my ear—I heard the ocean roar!
(Raise hands to ear.)

I found a tiny little shell one day, upon the ocean sand.
(Cup one hand as if holding a shell.)
The waves had worn it nice and smooth—it felt nice in my hand.
(Rub other hand over cupped hand.)

Tongue Twister

Our otter, Otto (*Say three time quickly.*)

Small-Group Activities

Over and Under

Using crepe paper streamers in a chain link fence or laundry basket, teach the children how to weave.

Old

Ask children, "What is old?" Their answers will be very interesting.

Ocean in a Bottle

Mix one part clear vegetable oil and three parts denatured alcohol in a medium-size clear plastic bottle. Add blue food coloring and glue the lid securely. Let the children twist and turn the bottle to create ocean waves.

Oatmeal

Help the children make oatmeal to have for a snack. Offer different flavorings such as vanilla or cinnamon, and raisins and berries for toppings.

Ovals

Provide a variety of ovals in different sizes and shapes. Ask the children to sort them by color or size.

P

Patrick—Name Story

Patrick is a painter. He paints on big sheets of white paper. Patrick prefers to paint pictures of animals. He paints panthers, panda bears, peacocks, and penguins. Sometimes Patrick will paint pictures of people, pumpkins, piñatas, planes, pianos, or pine trees. After Patrick finishes plenty of paintings, he picks one to show his brother.

Peanut Sitting on a Railroad Track

Song

(Tune: "Polly Wolly Doodle")

A peanut sat on a railroad track,
His heart was all a' flutter.
Then round the bend came a railroad train.
Toot! Toot! Peanut butter!
Squish!

Pease Porridge Hot

Poem

(Make up a partner clap.)
Pease porridge hot,
Pease porridge cold,
Pease porridge in the pot,
Nine days old.
Some like it hot.
Some like it cold.
Some like in the pot,
Nine days old!

Five Little Pumpkins

Finger Play

Five Little Pumpkins sitting on a gate.
(Hold up five fingers.)
First one said, "It's getting late."
(Wiggle first finger.)
Second one said, "There's something in the air."
(Wiggle second finger.)
Third one said, "We don't care."
(Wiggle third finger.)
Fourth one said, "Let's run, let's run."
(Wiggle fourth finger.)
Fifth one said, "Oh, it's just fun."
(Wiggle fifth finger.)
But whooo went the wind and out went the light
(Hold hands on both sides of your mouth and blow.)
And five little pumpkins rolled out of sight.
(Roll hand over hand.)

Tongue Twister

Puppy puddle (*Say three times quickly.*)

Small-Group Activities

Pet Parade

Have the children bring a stuffed animal to school. Make a leash for each pet and have a pet parade through the school.

Pin the Tail on the Pony

Provide a large pony shape and a pony tail. Play a game like Pin the Tail on the Donkey.

Pink Paper-Plate Pig

Paint a paper plate with pink tempera. Add pink paper triangle ears. Add eyes and a mouth. Glue on a pink cotton ball for a nose. Use two black hole punches for nostrils.

People in the Park

Provide chenille wires for the children to twist together to make people. Have the children build a park with blocks. Let the chenille-wire people play in the park.

Pyramid

Discuss the shape of a pyramid and show pictures or diagrams. Let the children build pyramids with blocks.

Qualeka—Name Story

Qualeka's family is Native American. She and her family go on quick trips on the weekends. One time they even went to Quebec ... that's in Canada! Sometimes they travel by train, which is quite nice because it's so quiet. Qualeka always takes her cozy quilt to take naps with on their trips. She also draws pictures of queens and ducks that quack.

Six White Ducks — Song

Six white ducks that I once knew,
Fat ducks, skinny ducks, they were, too.
But the one little duck with the feather on her back,
She ruled the others with a quack, quack, quack!
Down to the river they would go,
Wibble, wobble, wibble, wobble all in a row.
But the one little duck with the feather on her back,
She ruled the others with a quack, quack, quack!

Quiet Time — Finger Play

Let your hands go clap, clap, clap. *(Clap.)*
Let your feet go tap, tap, tap. *(Tap.)*
Fold your hands in your lap. *(Put hands in lap.)*
Don't go to sleep—it's not time to nap
(Shake head no.)
Do you know what time it is? *(Answer: Quiet Time)*

Be Very Quiet — Poem

Shhh—be very quiet,
Shhh—be very still.
Fold your busy little hands,
Close your sleepy little eyes.
Shhh—be very quiet.

Tongue Twister

Quilt quietly. (*Say three times quickly.*)

Small-Group Activities

Quarters in a Quart

Stand on a **Q** shape and toss quarters into quart containers. How many get in?

Quick Quencher

Discuss what it means to "quench" your thirst and when one might be thirsty. Provide cups, spoons, powdered drink mix, and water. Write the recipe with simple directions and picture clues for the children to follow.

Make It Quick

Provide a small jar with a lid, instant pudding, and milk. Put 1 tablespoon of pudding mix and 1/3 cup of milk in the jar. Shake it up for quick pudding.

Question Marks and Q's

Roll clay and make **?**'s and **Q**'s.

It's Quite Quiet Here

Have the class brainstorm a list of places that might be quiet. Some ideas might be a library, an empty building, the inside of a box, the top of a mountain, or the classroom when all the kids have left!

Ringo—Name Story

Ringo really likes rabbits. When his family moved from Japan to Rhode Island, Ringo received a pet rabbit. Ringo named the rabbit Rita because it is a girl rabbit. Ringo reads books about rabbits so he remembers how to take care of Rita. Rita's cage is red and has a round window. Ringo sometimes places an umbrella on the cage's roof to protect Rita from the rain.

Row, Row, Row Your Boat — Song

Row, row, row your boat
Gently down the stream.
Merrily, merrily, merrily, merrily,
Life is but a dream.

I Like Red — Poem

I like red. I like it a bunch.
I like red jam. I like red punch.
I like red flowers. I like red shoes.
Red is the color I always choose.
I like red. Red's the best.
I like red socks. I like red vests.
I like red hair. Oh, can't you see?
Red is the only color for me.

The Rabbit — Finger Play

Can you make a rabbit
(Hold up index and middle finger of one hand.)
With two ears so very long?
And let him hop and hop about
(Hop hand around.)
On legs so small and strong?

He nibbles, nibbles carrots
(Nibble with thumb and index finger.)
For his dinner every day.
As soon as he has had enough,
(Hide rabbit behind your back.)
He scampers far away.

Tongue Twister

Really ready *(Say three times quickly.)*

Small-Group Activities

Red Rocket

Glue red paper squares together to build a rocket. Cut triangles off some squares to make a nose and side wings. Add the blast-off fire.

Red Rubbings

Provide each child with lightweight paper and a red crayon from which the paper has been removed. Let the children experiment with different textures by laying the paper over a variety of surfaces and rubbing over the paper with the side of the crayon.

Remember the Row

Place three or four common objects in a row. Cover the objects with a cloth and remove one of the objects. Show the objects again and ask the children which object has been removed. As the children become proficient, increase the number of objects.

Rope Racing

Provide a jump rope for each child. Have the children lay out ropes straight and race to the end of the rope and back while running, walking backwards, crawling, walking with an eraser balanced on their heads, and so on.

Rainbow Rabbit

Color rainbow stripes to cover a 6" x 9" sheet of white paper. Trace a rabbit pattern on another sheet of colored paper and cut it out. Glue the outline of the rabbit over the rainbow.

Shalyn—Name Story

Shalyn lives in Syracuse, New York. She has a sister named Samantha and a brother named Sydney. In the summer, Shalyn and her siblings swim at the beach and build castles in the sand. They search for shells, sea horses, and sharks! Shalyn would like to learn how to sail and own a ship someday. Then she can siesta at sea!

A Sailor Went to Sea — Song

A sailor went to sea, sea, sea.
To see what she could see, see, see.
But all that she could see, see, see.
Was the bottom of the deep blue sea, sea, sea.

See-Saw, Millie McGraw — Poem

See-saw, Millie McGraw.
Rocking slow,
Back and forth we go.
See-saw, Millie McGraw.

Sometimes — Finger Play

Sometimes I am tall,
(Stand tall.)
Sometimes I am small.
(Crouch low.)
Sometimes I am very, very, tall.
(Stand on tiptoes.)
Sometimes I am very, very small.
(Crouch and lower head.)
Sometimes tall,
(Stand tall.)
Sometimes small.
(Crouch down.)
Sometimes neither tall or small.
(Stand normally.)

Tongue Twister

Sheep sleep. (*Say three times quickly.*)

Small-Group Activities

Sorting Sacks

Put a different colored mark on the outside of each of several plastic bags. Provide a bucket of small household or classroom items and have the children sort the items into bags by color.

Super Sun

Provide fingerpaint paper and yellow fingerpaint so the children can paint a large sun. Then ask each child to dictate a sentence about the sun.

Scoop Some Sand

Provide containers of various sizes and shapes, including several scoops. Allow the children to experiment with sand by pouring, sifting, and packing the sand.

Swing and Sway

Listen to the rhythm of music and swing and sway to the beat.

See If It Will Sink

Put items that will sink and items that will float at the water table or near a tub of water. Let children experiment with buoyancy.

Tristan—Name Story

Tristan is a terrific tennis player! He tries to practice on Tuesdays and Thursdays, but he always plays tennis on Saturdays. Tristan and his father, Thomas, travel into town after he plays tennis. They walk on trails to the park as they eat tangerine ice cream. Tristan and his dad like to talk about today's game and the fun times they share!

Three Straight Sides/ Tres lados rectos

Song

(Tune: Three Blind Mice)

Three straight sides,
Three straight sides,
See how they meet,
See how they meet,
They follow the path that a triangle makes,
Three straight sides and that's all that it takes,
Three straight sides,
Three straight sides.

Terrific Toes

Poem

I have such terrific toes,
I take them with me wherever I goes.
I have such fantastic feet,
No matter what, they still smell sweet.
Toes and feet and feet and toes.
There's nothing else as fine as those.

My Turtle

Finger Play

This is my turtle
(Make a fist—leave thumb outside.)
He lives in a shell
(Hide thumb in fist.)
He likes his home very well.
(Nod your head.)
He pokes his head out when he wants to eat
(Extend thumb.)
And pulls it back when he wants to sleep.
(Hide thumb in fist.)

Tongue Twister

Three throats (*Say three times quickly.*)

Small-Group Activities

Tear the Tape

Tape pieces of inexpensive masking tape or wrapping tape to a sheet of paper to make a design or picture. Paint over the whole paper with tempera. When it's dry, take off the tape and your picture will be waiting.

Try It with Toothpicks and Triangles

Create a collage with various sizes and colors of construction paper triangles and flat, wooden toothpicks.

Totally Terrific, ______!

Encourage a positive self-image by having the children draw self-portraits and dictate three attributes that make them "totally terrific." For example, "I share my toys," "I can run fast," "I have good ideas." Label the papers "Totally Terrific, (child's name)!"

Touch with Your Toes

On a poster, glue on several different textures: sandpaper, carpet, cotton, beans, waxed paper, cardboard bordette, fake fur fabric, and so on. Let the children explore with their toes.

Taste with Your Tongue

Provide examples of foods that are salty, sour, sweet, and bitter. Make a class graph of favorites.

U

Ulani—Name Story

Ulani lives in Hawaii. Her family lives near a university. Ulani and her family usually go for a bike ride after dinner. If it's unexpectedly sunny, Ulani prefers to sit under an umbrella instead. When her Uncle Ulysses visits from Utah, he plays his ukulele for all of them.

I Can Play the Ukulele

Song

(Tune: I've Been Working on the Railroad)

I can play the ukulele
All the livelong day
I can play the ukulele
To chase the blues away.

Can't you hear the strings a-strumming
From here to Cobbler's Run
Can't you hear the people humming
Please come and join the fun!

The Unicorn

Pam Schiller

Poem

The one animal I just adore
Is one I've never seen before
It looks a little like a horse
Except for its one long horn, of course.
It comes in only the color white
I dream of seeing it day and night.
So if a unicorn you happen to see
Whatever you do, please, please find me.

Uniquely Me

Pam Schiller

Finger Play

My mom says I'm uniquely me
(Point to self.)
I look in the mirror 'cause I want to see.
(Hold palm up like a mirror.)
Here are my eyes, nose, mouth, and hair
(Point to each body part.)
But nothing I see appears to be rare.
(Shake head.)

I look around at all my friends
(Look at friends.)
And think about what makes them friends
Then I know what I'm looking for
(Hold finger up like you just thought of something.)
Unique is what makes you who you are.

It's what you say and what you do
(Turn right palm up, then left palm.)
That makes you ...uniquely you!
(Point to self.)

Tongue Twister

Upset uncles (*Say three times quickly.*)

Small-Group Activities

Uniforms

Gather uniforms and place them in the Dramatic Play Center.

Ukulele Fun

Invite a guest to come to the classroom to play the ukulele.

Unicorn Hunt

Hide a stuffed unicorn or a picture of one and see who can find it the quickest.

What Makes Me Unique?

Ask the children what makes them really unique. Encourage them to draw a picture of what makes them unique.

Unicorn Ring Toss

Use a cone to represent a unicorn horn. Provide plastic rings and invite the children to try to toss the rings over the horn.

Vincente—Name Story

Vincente is very helpful. He volunteers with his mother, Valerie, to recycle newspapers, cans, bottles, and plastic. For his mom's birthday, Vincente gave her a vase filled with violets. She thanked Vincente and told him that they were going to Vermont for vacation. They would drive in a van to visit family friends, play volleyball, and have fun!

Five Little Ducks

Song

Five little ducks went out one day,
Over the hills and far away.
Papa duck called with a "Quack, quack, quack."
Four little ducks came swimming back.
(Repeat, losing one more duck each time until you are left with one duck. Have Mama Duck call and end with "Five little ducks came swimming back.")

My Little Valentine

Poem

I made a little Valentine.
I made it by myself.
I love my little Valentine
I made all by myself.

Now if you want to make one too,
Get some paper, lace, and glue.
Write "I Love You" across its face,
Glue on glitter and some lace.

Now you can make a Valentine.
You can make it by yourself.
You'll love your little Valentine
You made all by yourself.

Five Fancy Valentines

Finger Play

(Hold up five fingers and put them down as valentines disappear.)
Five fancy valentines in the card store,
Austin bought one, then there were four.
Four fancy valentines, sweet as can be,
Sam bought one, then there were three.
Three fancy valentines waiting for you,
Madison bought one, now there are two.
Two fancy valentines you better run,
Gabby's buying one, soon there'll be none.

Tongue Twister

Valuable valentine (*Say three times quickly.*)

Small-Group Activities

A Very Important Vote

Discuss the important privilege of voting in our country. Have the class vote on something that you really don't mind their choosing, such as a choice of snacks.

Violins, Violins

Play a variety of violin music. Show a picture of a violin. If possible, have a visitor come in and play the violin for the class.

Very Important Visitor

Invite special visitors to discuss their jobs.

Violets on a Vine

Turn a rectangular sheet of paper horizontally and draw a wavy, green line across the paper. Add leaves and purple flowers.

Vinegar Volcano

Display colorful pictures of volcanic eruptions. Let the children create imaginary eruptions by mixing 6 tsp. of vinegar in a cup and carefully adding 1 tsp. of baking soda. Watch out!

Walai—Name Story

Walai enjoys writing. Sometimes, while watching birds outside her window, Walai wonders about animals she has never seen. Then, she writes about them ... wolves, whales, woodpeckers, walruses, and wombats. She especially likes to write about winter with its white snow and windy days. Walai thinks writing, wildlife, and winter are wonderful!

The Wheels on the Bus — Song

The wheels on the bus go round and round.
(Move hands in circular motion.)
Round and round, round and round.
The wheels on the bus go round and round,
All around the town.
(Extend arms up and out.)

The windshield wipers go swish, swish, swish.
(Sway hands back and forth.)
The baby on the bus goes, "Wah, wah, wah."
(Rub eyes.)
People on the bus go up and down
(Stand up, sit down.)
The horn on the bus goes beep, beep, beep.
(Pretend to beep horn.)
The money on the bus goes clink, clink, clink.
(Drop in change.)
The driver on the bus says, "Move on back."
(Make hitchhiking movement.)

Whether the Weather — Poem

Whether the weather be fine,
Or whether the weather be not,
Whether the weather be cold,
Or whether the weather be hot,
We'll weather the weather
Whatever the weather,
Whether we like it or not.

I Wiggle — Finger Play

I wiggle, wiggle, wiggle my fingers.
(Wiggle fingers.)
I wiggle, wiggle, wiggle my toes.
(Wiggle toes.)
I wiggle, wiggle, wiggle my shoulders.
(Wiggle shoulders.)
I wiggle, wiggle, wiggle my nose.
(Wiggle nose.)

Tongue Twister

Which wish (*Say three times quickly.*)

Small-Group Activities

Willing Workers

Assign groups of children different cleaning jobs in the room. The children can wash tabletops, dust the shelves, fold the dress-up and doll clothes, and pick up items. You might play "Whistle While You Work" as background music.

Waiters and Waitresses

Provide aprons, note pads, pencils, menus, napkins, trays, and paper or plastic dishes. Let the children set up a table and chairs like those in a restaurant. Have them take turns role-playing waiters and waitresses. Discuss things they might say.

What's in the Web?

Draw a web on black paper with white chalk and add a friendly spider with chalk or crayons.

Would You Weigh It?

Provide balance scales and a variety of objects. Have the children weigh the objects and put them in order from heaviest to lightest.

Xavier—Name Story

Xavier and his family are moving from Florida to Texas. They have several boxes to pack. They labeled each box so their belongings don't get mixed up. Xavier's parents are going to fix the garage door before the new family moves in. Xavier's family has only six days left in Florida. Their new house will have extra space for a pet, but not a fox! Everyone is excited to move to Texas.

Six White Ducks

Song

Six white ducks that I once knew,
Fat ducks, skinny ducks, they were, too.
But the one little duck with the feather on her back,
She ruled the others with a quack, quack, quack!
Down to the river they would go,
Wibble, wobble, wibble, wobble all in a row.
But the one little duck with the feather on her back,
She ruled the others with a quack, quack, quack!

A Fox and an Ox

Poem

A fox and an ox
Sitting in a box,
Playing the sax
All the livelong day.

Said the fox to the ox
Sitting in a box,
It's a quarter to six,
Let's be on our way.

X Marks the Spot

Finger Play

Pam Schiller

Make an X just like this,
(Make an X with fingers.)
Mark the spot so you won't miss.
Stand back, take aim,
(Close one eye as if determining aim.)
Toss the beanbag—win the game.
(Pretend to toss beanbag.)

Tongue Twister

Extra exits (*Say three times quickly.*)

Small-Group Activities

Tyrannosaurus Rex

Read books about Tyrannosaurus rex and show pictures. Have children make their own Tyrannosaurus rex with paint, crayons, or markers.

What's in the Box?

Provide a box with an object hidden inside. Have the children ask questions that can be answered with *yes* or *no* to get clues to "What's in the box?"

What Comes Next?

Provide patterns of colors, shapes, or simple pictures. Have children determine what comes next. These are easy to make into folder games.

Taxi! Taxi!

Set up chairs to simulate the seats in a car. Let the children play that they're riding in a taxi. They can take turns being the driver. The driver can use a clock or stopwatch to time the ride and charge one penny or one token for each minute.

X Puzzles

Cut several large **X**'s out of tagboard and laminate them. Cut each **X** into a different puzzle. Have the children put the puzzles together.

Y

Yasmeen—Name Story

Yasmeen was thinking about her friends back home yesterday. Yasmeen and her family are from Yemen. Right now, they live in Yates City, Illinois. Fortunately, Yasmeen and her family are going back to visit Yemen this year. Yasmeen likes to pack her yellow suitcase for trips because her yarn and crafts always fit inside. Yasmeen's father tells her when they are leaving. Yasmeen yells with excitement, "I can't wait!"

You Are My Sunshine

Song

You are my sunshine, my only sunshine.
You make me happy when skies are gray.
You'll never know, dear, how much I love you.
Please don't take my sunshine away.

I Had a Little Yo-Yo

Poem

Tiffany Markle

I had a little yo-yo
It was my favorite toy
I played with it quite often
When I was just a boy
I used to know a trick or two
You could even say a few
But none that I remember now
Much less could even do.

Yarn Trick

Finger Play

Pam Schiller

(Suit actions to words.)
Take a piece of yarn
Tie it around your finger
Now you won't forget
What you need to remember.

Tongue Twister

Yellow yo-yos (*Say three times quickly.*)

Small-Group Activities

Yodeling You

Listen to recordings of yodeling and discuss why people yodel in the mountains. Let the children practice yodeling. Then have each child pair with a partner and yodel on a cue from his or her partner.

The Young Ones

Brainstorm and list names of several animals. Have children name their young: goose-gosling, hen-chick, cow-calf, dog-puppy, duck-duckling, horse-foal, deer-fawn, cat-kitten, pig-piglet, kangaroo-joey.

Yard of Yellow Yarn

Help the children measure yellow yarn into 1-yard lengths. Let the children create pictures on paper using the yarn either whole or in pieces. The children may use crayons to add to the picture.

You Must Yield

Discuss shapes and meanings of various road signs. Provide paper roads with intersections appropriate for yield signs. Provide wooden road signs and cars to role-play yielding for other cars.

Z

Zack—Name Story

Zack wanted to start a collection, but he couldn't think of what he liked the most. His sister Zoe collects basketball cards, and his parents collect coins. Then, finally, Zack remembered what his favorite thing was. While he and his family were at the zoo, they saw lions, seals, elephants, bears, giraffes, alligators, and birds. But Zack's favorite animal was the zebra. Now he collects zebra stickers, zebra toys, and zebra pictures.

Oats, Peas, Beans

Song

Oats, peas, beans, and barley grows.
Oats, peas, beans, and barley grows.
Not you nor I or anyone knows,
How oats, peas, beans, and barley grows!

The Zebra

Poem

Pam Schiller

The zebra looks just like a horse
Except for all those stripes, of course.
I wonder if he's black with stripes of snowy white—
Or is he snowy white with stripes as black as night?

My Zipper Suit

Finger Play

(Traditional)

This zipper suit is bunny brown.
(Hold arms out to side.)
The top zips up, the legs zip down.
(Zip top up and the legs down.)
I wear it every day.
My Daddy brought it from downtown.
Zip it up, zip it down.
(Run zippers up and down.)
And hurry out to play.
(Turn around.)

Tongue Twister

Zero zebras (*Say three times quickly.*)

Small-Group Activities

Let's Go to the Zoo

Discuss the changing role of zoos today as they work to protect endangered species. Compare cages with natural types of habitats found in modern zoos. Display a variety of zoo pictures in the room. Plan a class field trip to a nearby zoo.

Zigzag Zebra

Paste black paper zigzags on a large white **Z.** Add an eye and strips of paper for legs and a tail.

Zeros, Zigzags and Zs

Provide shallow trays with a thin layer of sand. Have children draw zeros, zigzags, Zs, and write the word *zoo* in the sand tray.

Zip to Zero

Provide 10 counters and 1 die for each child. Taking turns, have each child roll a die and take away that many counters. The child who gets to zero first is the winner.

Zoom, Zoom, Zoom!

Brainstorm and list things that go *zoom.* Let the children illustrate their favorite one and add the word *zoom!*

Word Lists

Consonants in the Initial Position

Bb as /b/

bad
bag*
bait
bake
ball*
ban
band*
bank*
bar
barn*
base
bask
bat*
batch
bath*
bathe
beach*
beak*
beam
bean*
bear*
beast
beat
bed*
bee*
beech
beef
been
beep
beet*
beg
bell*
belt*
bend
bent
best
bet
big
bike*
bill
bin*
bind
birch
bird*
bit
bite
boar*
boast
boat*
bog
boil
bold
bolt*
bone*
book*
boom
boost
bop
born
boss
both
bow*
bowl*
box*
boy*
buck
bud*
bug*
bull*
bum
bump*
bunch
bunk*
bunt
burn
bus*
but
buy
buzz
by

Cc as /k/

cab*
cage*
call
came
camp
can*
cane*
cap*
cape*
car*
card*
care
cart*
case
cash
cast*
cat*
cave*
coal
coast
coat*
cob*
cod
coil
coin*
cold
colt*
comb*
come
cone*
cool
cope
cord
corn*
cost
cot*
cough
could
count
court
cove
cow*
cub*
cube*
curl*
curve
cut
cute

Dd as /d/

dab
damp
dash
date
dawn
day
deaf
deal
deck*
deep
deer*
den
dent*
desk*
dew
die
dig*
dike*
dill
dim
dime*
dine
ding
dip
dirt
dish*
disk*
dive*
do
dock*
doe*
dog*
doll*
dome
done
door*
dose
down
doze
duck*
due
dug
dull
dump
dune
dunk
dusk
dust
dye

Ff as /f/

face*
fact
fad
fade
fail
faint
fair
fake
fall*
false
fame
fan*
far
farm*
fast
fate
feast
fed
feed
feel
fell
fence*
few
fib
fig*
fight
file*
film*
fine
fire*
first
fish*
fist*
fit
five*
foam*
foe
foil
fold
folk
fond
food
fool
foot*
for
force
form
fort*
four*
fowl
fox*
fun
fur
fuse
fuzz

Gg as /g/

gain
game*
gap
gas*
gasp
gate*
gave
gaze
gear
geese*
get
gift*
gill
girl*
give
go
goal
goat*
goes
gold
golf*
gone
good
goof
goose*
gulp
gull
gum*
gush
gust

Hh as /h/

hair*
half
hall*
halt
ham*
hand*
hang
hard
hare*
has
hat*
hate
have
hay*
he
head*
heal
hear
heart*
heat
heel*
help
hem
her
here
high
hill*
him
hip
his
hit
hive*
hoe*
hog*
hold
hole*
home*
hood*
hoof*
hook*
hop*
hope
horn*
horse*
hose*
hot
house*
how
hum
hung
hunt
hurl
hurt
husk*
hut*

* picturable

Word Lists

Jj as /j/

jab
jacks*
jade
jail
jam*
jar*
jaw*
jay*
jeans*
jeep*
jerk
jet*
jib
jig
job
jog
join
joint
joke
jolt
joy
jug*
juice
July
jump
June
junk
jury
just

Kk as /k/

kale
keel
keen
keep
keg*
kelp
kept
key*
kid*
kill
kilt*
kind
king*
kiss*
kit*
kite*

Ll as /l/

lab
lace*
lack
lad
lag
laid
lake*
lamp*
land
lane*
lap
lash
last
latch
late
leaf*
leak
lean
leap*
least
leaves*
left
leg*
lend
less
lest
let
lick*
life
lift
light*
like
limp
line*
link
lion*
lip*
list
lit
live
loaf*
loam
loan
loaves*
log*
lone
long
look
loose
lose
lot
love
luck
lug
lump
lunch

Mm as /m/

mad*
made
maid
mail*
main
make
man*
map*
march*
March
mare
mark
Mars
mash*
mask*
mast*
mat*
match*
math
May
maze*
me
meal
mean
means
meat
meet
melt
men*
mend
mess
met
mice*
mid
might
mike*
mile
milk*
mill
mind
mine
mint
miss
mist
mix
moan
moat*
mob
mold
mole*
mom
moo
mood
moon*
mop*
mope
more
moss
moth
mouse*
mouth*
move
mow*
much
mud
muff*
mug*
mule*
mumps
mush
must
mutt
my

Nn as /n/

nab
nag
nail*
name
nap
near
neck*
need
nest*
net*
new
next
nice
nick
night*
nip
nix
no
nod
noise
north
nose*
not
note*
now
nub
nurse*
nut*

Pp as /p/

pad*
page*
pain
paint*
pal
pale
pan*
pant
pants*
pass
past
pat*
patch*
paw*
pay
pea*
peach*
peaks*
pear*
pearl*
peck
peel*
peek
peg*
pen*
pet*
pie*
pig*
pike
pill*
pin*
pine*
pint
pit
pod*
point*
poke
pole*
pond*
pork
port
post
pour
puff
pull
punt
purse*
push
put
putt

Qq as /q/

quack
quail*
quake
quart
quarter*
queen*
quick
quiet
quill*
quilt*
quirk
quit
quite
quiz

Rr as /r/

race
rack
rag*
rail*
rain*
raise
rake*
ram*
ramp*
ran
ranch
range
rank
rap
rat*
rate
rave
raw
ray
real
red*
rent
rib
rich
ride
rig
right
rim
ring*
rink
rip
ripe
rise
road*
roast
rob
robe*
rock*
rod
roll
roof*
room*
root*
rope*
rose*
rot
round
row
rub
rude
rug*
rule
run
rush
rust
rut

Ss as /s/

sack*
sad*
safe*
sag
sage
said
sail*
sake
sale
salt*
same
sand*
sang
sap
sat
save
saw*

* picturable

say
sea*
see
seed*
seek
seem
seen
seep
self
sell
send
sent
serve
set
seven*
sew*
sick*
side
sieve*
sigh
sight
sign
silk
sill
sing
sink*
sip
sir
sit
size
so
soak
soap*
soar
sock*
sod
soft
soil
some
son
song
soon
soot
sore
sort
soul
sound
soup*
sour
south
sow
sub
such
suit*
sum
sun*
surf*

Tt as /t/

tab
tack*
tag*
tail*
take
talk
tall
tame
tan
tap*
tape*
tar
tea*
teach
team
tear
tease
tee*
teen
tell
ten*
tick
tide
tie*
till
time
tin
tip
tire*
to
toad*
toe*
toll
ton
tone
tool
top*
tore
torn
toss
touch
tough
tour
tow
town
toy*
tub*
tube*
tuck
tug*
tune
turn

Vv as /v/

vain
van*
vane*
vase*
vat
vault*
veal
veil*
vein
vent*
verse
very
vest*
view
vine*
vise*
voice
vote*

Ww as /w/

wad
wade
wag
wage
wagon*
waist
wait
wake
walk
wall*
wand*
want
warm
warn
wash*
wasp*
waste
watch*
water*
wave*
wax
way
we
weak
wealth
wear
weave*
web*
weed
week
weep
weigh
weird
weld*
well*
went
west
wet
wick
wide
wife
wig*
wild
will
wilt
win*
wind*
wing*
wink*
wipe
wire
wise
wish
wit
with
woke
wolf*
won
wood*
wool
word
work
world
worm*
worry
worst
would

Yy as /y/

yacht*
yak*
yam*
yank
yard*
yawn*
year
yeast
yell
yes
yield
yoke*
yolk*
you
young
your
yowl
yuck

Zz as /z/

zag
zap
zebra*
zero*
zest
zinc
zing
zip
zone
zonk
zoo*
zoom

Consonants in the Final Position

b as /b/

cab*
club*
cob*
crab*
crib*
cub*
drab
flub
glob
grab
grub
hub
jab
job
lab
lob
mob
rib
rob
rub
scrub
shrub*
slab
snub
sob
stab
stub
sub
swab
tab
tub*
web*

d as /d/

bad
bead*
bed*
bid
bird*
braid*
bread*
cloud*
cod
fad
fed
feed*
food*
freed
glad
good
greed
hid
kid
laid
lead
lid*
load
mad*
mood
need
nod
pad
paid
plead
plod
raid
read*
red*
rid
road*
rod*
sad*
said
seed*
sled*
slid*
sod
speed
spud*
stead
steed
stood
toad*
wed
weed
wood
word

f as /f/

beef
brief
chef*
chief*
deaf
goof
grief
hoof*
leaf*
loaf*
proof*
reef*
roof*
spoof*

g as /g/

bag*
beg
big
bog
bug*
chug
clog

* picturable

dig*
dog*
drag
dug
fig*
flag*
fog
frog*
hog*
hug
jig
jug*
keg
lag
log*
lug
mug*
nag
peg*
pig*
plug*
rag*
rig
rug*
sag
shag
shrug
smug
snag
snug
tag*
tug*
twig*
wag
wig*

k as /k/

beak*
bike*
bleak
book*
break
brook*
leak
look
oak
peak
peek
seek
shook
soak
steak*
took
weak
week

l as /l/

bail
coal*
fail
goal*
hail
jail*
mail*
meal*
nail*
pail*
sail*
seal*
steal*
steel*
tail*
veil*
wheel*

n as /n/

ban
bean*
been
bin*
brain
can*
chain*
clean
corn*
den*
drain*
fan*
fin*
flown
fun
gain
gown
green*
grin
hen*
in
main
man*
men*
moon*
pain
pan*
pen*
pin*
plan
rain*
ran
run
seen
skin
spin
spoon*
sun*
tan
ten*
then
thin
tin
train*
twin*
when
win

p as /p/

cap*
cheap
chip
chop
clip
crop
cup*
deep
drip*
drop
flap
flip
flop
hip
hop*
jeep*
keep
lap
lip*
map*
mop*
nap
rap
rip
sap
sheep*
sip
skip
sleep*
slip
snap
soap*
stop*
sweep*
tap
tip
top*
trap
trip
up
weep
whip*
wrap
zip

t as /t/

bat*
beat
beet*
bet
bit
boat*
boot*
but
cat*
cheat
coat*
cot*
cut
dot*
feet*
fit
flat
float
foot*
get
goat*
got
great
greet
hat
heat
hit
hot
hut*
jet*
kit*
let
lit
lot
mat*
meat*
meet
met
moat*
neat
net*
not
nut*
paint*
pat
pet*
pit*
pleat
point
pot*
put
quit
rat*
rot
rut
sat
seat
set
sheet
shut
sit
sleet
spot*
suit*
sweet
wait
wet
what
wheat*
yet

x as /ks/

box*
fix
flax
fox*
lox
mix
sax*
six*
tax

Vowels

Long Vowels

a-e /ā/ as in *cake*

Note: Do not use **-ale** or **-are.**

ace
age
bake
base*
blade*
blame
blaze
brace
brake
brave
cage*
cake*
came
cane* (can*)
cape* (cap*)
case
cave*
chase
crane*
crate*
date
daze
drake
drape*
face*
fade (fad)
fake
fame
fate (fat)
flake*
flame*
frame*
gage (gag)
game*
gate*
gave
gaze
glaze
grace
grade
grape*
grate*
haste
hate (hat*)
haze
jade
lace*
lake*
lame
lane*
late
made (mad)
make
mane* (man*)
mate (mat*)
name
pace
page*
pane (pan*)
paste (past)
pave
place
plane* (plan)
plate*
quake
race*
rage (rag*)
rake*
rate (rat*)
rave
safe*
sake
same (Sam)
sane
save
shade* (shad)
shape
shave*
skate*
slate* (slat)
snake*
space
stage* (stag)
stake*
state
take
tame
tape* (tap)
taste

* picturable
( ) short vowel change

trace
trade
vane (van*)
vase*
wade (wad)
wage (wag)
wake
waste
wave

ai /ā/ as in *bait*

Note: Do not use **-ail** or **-air.**

aim (am)
bait (bat*)
braid* (brad)
brain* (bran)
chain*
claim (clam*)
drain*
faint
faith
grain*
laid (lad)
lain
maid* (mad)
main (man*)
paid (pad*)
pain (pan*)
paint* (pant)
plain (plan)
raid
rain* (ran)
stain (Stan)
strain
train*
vain (van*)
waist
wait

ay /ā/ as in *day*

bay
clay*
day
gray
hay*
lay*
may
pay
play
ray
say
spray*
stay
sway
tray*
way

ee /ē/ as in *feet*

Note: Do not use **-eel** or **-eer.**

bee*
beech
beef*
beep
beet* (bet)
cheek*
cheep
creep
deed
deep
fee
feed (fed)
feet*
free
greed
green*
greet
heed
jeep*
keep
meet (met)
need (Ned)
peek
peep (pep)
queen*
reef*
screech
screen*
see
seed*
seem
seen
seep
sheep*
sheet*
sleep*
sleet*
speech
speed (sped)
street*
sweep*
sweet
teen (ten*)
teeth*
three*
tree*
weed (wed)
week

ea /ē/ as in *team*

Note: Do not use **-eal** or **-ear.**

beach*
bead* (bed*)
beak*
beam
bean* (Ben)
beat (bet)
bleach
bleak
cheap
clean
cream*
dream
each
east
eat*
feast
flea*
gleam
heap
heat
jeans*
leaf*
leak
lean
leash*
least
mean (men*)
meat* (met)
neat (net*)
pea*
peach*
peak
plead
pleat
reach
scream
seam
seat* (set)
sneak
speak
stream*
tea
teach
team
weak
wheat*
yeast

i-e /ī/ as in *ice*

Note: Do not use **-ile** or **-ire.**

bike*
bite (bit)
chime
chive
dike*
dime* (dim)
dine
dive
drive
fine (fin)
five*
grime (grim)
hide (hid)
hive*
ice*
kite* (kit*)
life
like
lime*
line*
live
mice*
mine
nice
nine*
pike
pine* (pin)
price
rice*
ride (rid)
rise
shine (shin)
side
size
slice
slide* (slid)
spice
spike*
splice
stride
strive
tide
time (Tim)
twice
whine
white
wide
wife
wise

oa /ō/ as in *boat*

Note: Do not use **-oal** or **-oar.**

boat*
coach
coast (cost)
coat* (cot*)
float
foam
goat* (got)
groan
load
loaf*
loam
loan
moan
moat*
road* (rod)
roam
roast
soak
soap* (sop)
throat*
toad* (Tod)
toast

o-e / _ / as in *bone*

Note: Do not use **-ole** or **-ore.**

bone*
broke
choke
chose
clone
clothe (cloth*)
clothes*
clove
code (cod)
cone*
cope
cove
dome
dose
doze
drove
froze
globe* (glob)
grove
home*
hope (hop*)
hose*
joke
lone
nose*
note* (not)
phone*
poke
pose
robe* (rob)
rode (rod)
rope*
rose*
slope (slop)
smoke*
spoke*
stone*
stroke
those
throne*
tone
vote*
woke
yoke*
zone*

u-e /ū/ as in *tune*

Note: Do not use **-ule** or **-ure.**

chute*
crude
cube* (cub*)
cute (cut)
dune
flute*
fume
fuse*
huge (hug)
June
lute*
mute
prune*
rude
spruce
tube* (tub*)
tune
use (us)

Short Vowels

a /a/ as in *cat*

Note: Avoid using **(a)l, (a)r,** or **(a)w.**

act
add
am
as
at
back*
bad
bag*
ban
band*
bask
bat*
batch
bath*
black*
blast
bran
branch*
brand*
brass
cab*
camp
can*

* picturable
( ) short vowel change

Word Lists

cap*
cast*
cat*
catch
champ
chat
clam*
clamp
clan
clap*
clash
class
crack*
craft
cramp
crash
dab
dad
damp
dash
drag
fact
fad
fan*
fast
fat
flag*
flap
flash
flat
gap
gas*
gasp
glad
glass*
grab
grand
grant
graph*
grass*
had
ham*
hand*
has
hash
hat*
hatch
jack*
jam
lack
lad
lag
lamp*
land
lap
lash
last
latch
mad
man*
map*
mash
mask*
mass
mast
mat*
match*
math
nag
nap
pack*
pad
pan*
pant
pants*
pass
past
pat
patch*
path*
plan
plant
quack
rack
rag
ram
ramp
ran
rant
rap
rash
rat*
sack*
sad*
sag
sand
sap
sat
scratch*
slab
slack
slam
slant
snap*
span
splash
stack
stamp*
stand
strand
tab
tack*
tag*
tan
tap
task
than
that
track*
trap
van
vat
wag
yam*

e /e/ as in *set*

Note: Avoid using **(e)l**, **(e)r**, or **(e)w**.

bed*
beg
bench*
bend
best
bet
blend
bless
cent
chess*
chest*
crest
deck*
desk*
dress*
egg*
elf*
elm
end
fed
fresh
help
hem
hen*
jet*
kept
left
lend
less
lest
let
mend
mesh
mess
met
neck
nest*
net*
peg*
pet
press
red*
rest
send
set
sled*
slept
spend
spent
stem*
step*
stress
ten
tent
test
vest*
vet
web*
wept
west
wet
yet

i /i/ as in *sit*

Note: Avoid using **(i)l**, **(i)r**, or **(i)w**.

bib*
bid
big
bit
blimp
blink
brick*
chick*
chin*
click
clip
crib*
crisp
did
dig*
dim
dip
dish*
disk*
drink*
drip*
fib
fin*
fish*
fist*
fit
fix
flick
flip
gift*
gig
glint
hid
him
hip
his
hiss
hit
in
ink*
inn
is
it
kick
kin
kiss
lick
lift
lips*
list*
lit
miss
mix
pick*
pig*
pin*
pink*
pit
rib
rich
rid
rig
rim
rip
shift
ship*
sink*
sip
sit
six*
skin
skip
skit
slick
slid
slim
slip
splint*
sprint
stick*
stink
swim*
thin
think
this
tick
tip
trick
trim
trip
which
whip*
wick
wig*
win
wink
wish
wit
zip

o /o/ as in *cot*

Note: Avoid using **(o)l**, **(o)r**, or **(o)w**.

block*
blot
bop
box*
chop
clock*
clop
cob*
cod
cot*
crop
dock*
dot*
drop
flock
flop
fox*
got
hop
hot
job
lob
lock*
lot
mob
mom
mop*
nod
not
on
ox
plod
plot
pod
pond*
pop
pot*
rob
rock*
rod
rot
shock
shop
shot
slop
slot
sob
sock*
sod
sop
spot*
stop
top*
trot

* picturable

u /u/ as in *cup*

Note: Avoid using **(u)l**, **(u)r**, or **(u)w**.

bluff
blunt
blush
brush
buck
bud*
buff
bug*
bum
bump*
bunch
bunt
bus*
but
buzz
chunk
club*
clump
clunk
clutch
crust*
cub*
cuff*
cup*
cut
drug
drum*
duck*
dug
dump
dunk
dusk
dust
fluff
fun
fuss
fuzz
glum
grub
gruff
gum*
gust
hug*
hum
hunt
hush
husk
jug*
jump*
just
luck
lug
lump
much
mud*
muff*
mug*
mush
must
mutt
nut*
pluck
plug*
plum*
plus
puff*
pump*
punt
putt*
rub
ruff
rug*
run
runt
rush
rust
rut
shrub
shun
shut
skunk*
slug*
slump
snub
snug
struck
strum
stub
stuck
stump*
sub
such
suds*
sum
sun*
truck*
trunk*
tub*
tuck
tug*
tusk*
up
us

Dolch 95 Common Nouns

airplane
apple
baby
back
ball
barn
basket
bear
bed
bell
bird
birthday
boat
book
box
boy
bread
bus
cake
cap
car
cat
chair
chicken
children
coat
corn
cow
dog
doll
door
duck
egg
elephant
eye
farm
farmer
father
feet
fire
fish
floor
flower
garden
girl
grandfather
grandmother
grass
hand
head
hen
hill
horse
house
kitten
leg
letter
man
men
milk
money
monkey
mother
nest
nose
paper
party
picture
pig
pony
puppy
rabbit
rain
ring
road
school
sheep
shoe
snow
squirrel
stick
store
street
sun
table
tail
top
toy
train
tree
wagon
watch
water
window
wood

* picturable

Rhyming Words Memory Game

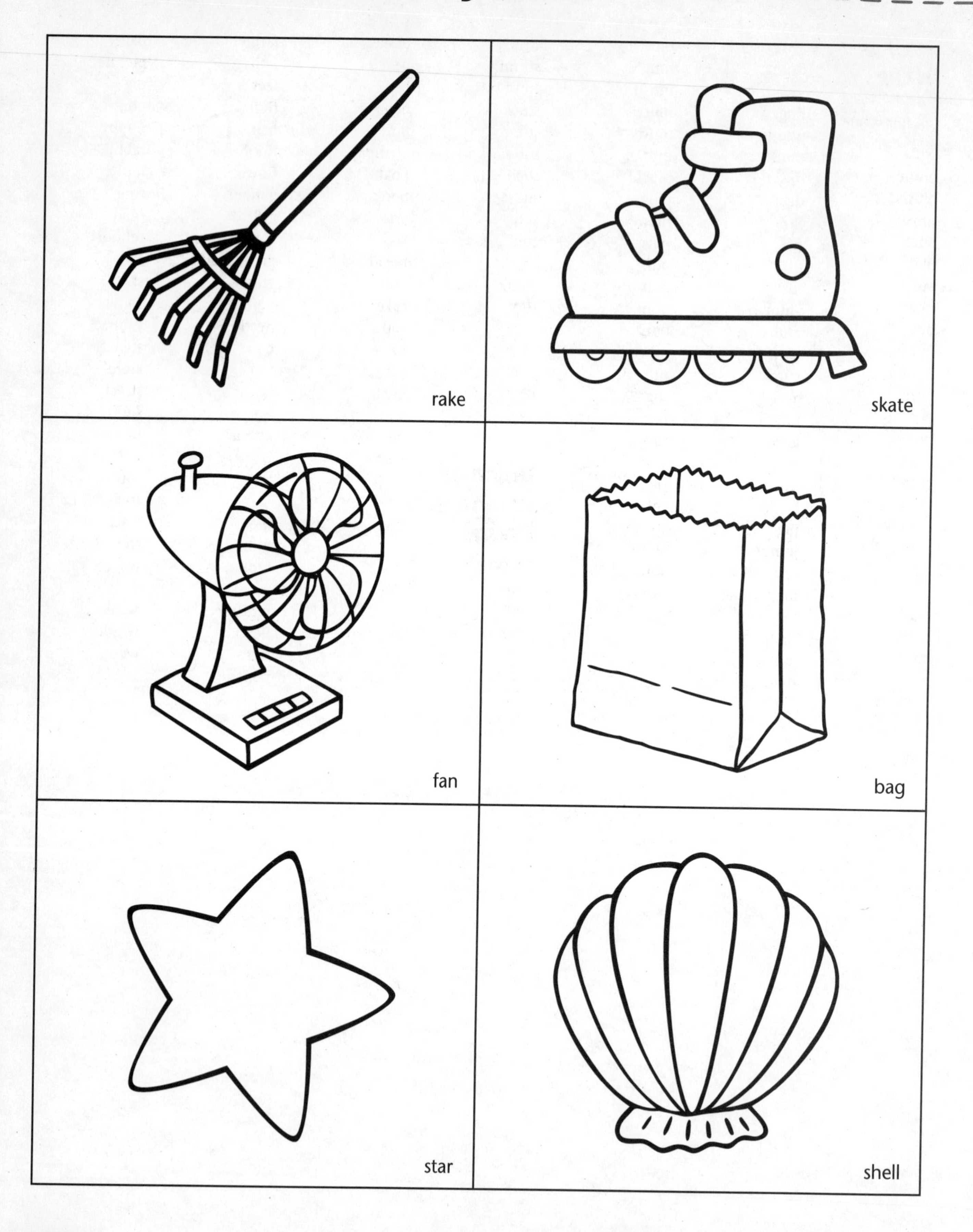

Make copies, color, and laminate for games suggested in the ***DLM Early Childhood Express Teacher's Editions.***

Make copies, color, and laminate for games suggested in the
DLM Early Childhood Express Teacher's Editions.

Rhyming Heart Puzzles

Make copies, color, and laminate for games suggested in the ***DLM Early Childhood Express Teacher's Editions.***

Make copies, color, and laminate for games suggested in the
DLM Early Childhood Express Teacher's Editions.

Make copies, color, and laminate for games suggested in the
DLM Early Childhood Express Teacher's Editions.